The Usborne Little Children's
CHRISTMAS
Activity Book

James Maclaine
and Lucy Bowman

Designed and illustrated by
Erica Harrison

Laurent Kling, Fred Blunt, Anni Betts,
Erica Sirotich, Emily Balsley
and Maria Neradova

Edited by Fiona Watt

You'll find the answers to the
puzzles on pages 61-64.

Festive spotting

How many of these
things can you find in
the branches?

 .... red hearts

 .... fir cones

 .... snowflakes

 .... candy canes

 .... white doves

 .... bells

 .... gold stars

 .... spotty decorations

3

Christmas shopping

Decorate the windows of this department store. Place each sticker from the sticker pages over the label it matches.

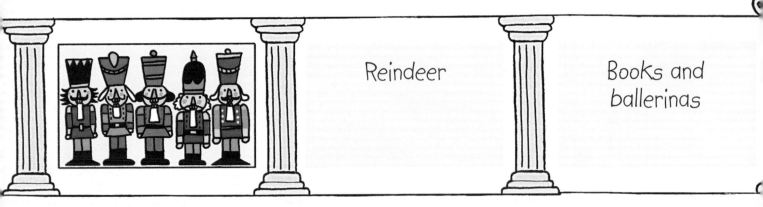

Reindeer

Books and ballerinas

Which car has the most shopping? Draw an 'X' on it.

How many of these things can you spot?

 red bags ....

 Santa hats ....

White
Christmas

Teddy bears'
party

Red and
gold

I've dropped a bag.
Can you find it?

 rolls of
wrapping ....
paper

green ....
bags

 pigeons ....

Christmas colouring

Fill in the decorations with pens
that match the coloured spots.

Santa's grotto

The children are waiting patiently to see Santa. Can you spot...?

- a clock
- an elf in a floppy hat
- two shopping bags
- a yellow star
- a sleeping baby
- a spotty scarf
- a mouse

Colour in the decorations on this tree.

How many presents can
you spot altogether? ....

SANTA
THIS WAY

Cool creatures

These animals all live in cold places on Earth.

How many polar bears can
you count hiding in the snow?   ....

Can you spot five differences between these fur seals?

Which way should the Arctic fox go to reach its den?

How to draw a swimming penguin

1. Draw an oval for its body.

2. Add an eye and a patch on its tummy.

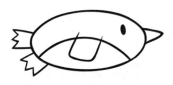

3. Draw on its beak, feet and flipper.

Draw more penguins swimming under the ice and colour them in.

Sweet treats

This jar is filled with pairs of matching candy canes, except for one. Draw an 'X' on the candy cane that isn't one of a pair.

Which square is missing from the jar below?

A   B   C

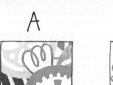 

Decorate these Christmas cookies using the stickers from the sticker pages.

Santa's workshop

All the elves are busy in the workshop, but one is taking a nap. Can you spot the sleeping elf somewhere on these pages?

Whose apron is whose? Draw lines between the elves and their aprons.

Draw circles around five differences between these two robots.

What type of present does each machine make? Change the order of the letters and write in the correct words.

ibek

_ _ _ _ _ _

lodl

_ _ _ _

kobo

_ _ _ _

Are there more wrapped or unwrapped presents on this bench?

.... wrapped presents

.... unwrapped presents

Perfect presents

Can you guess what's inside each present?
Stick the stickers from the sticker pages
over the shapes they match.

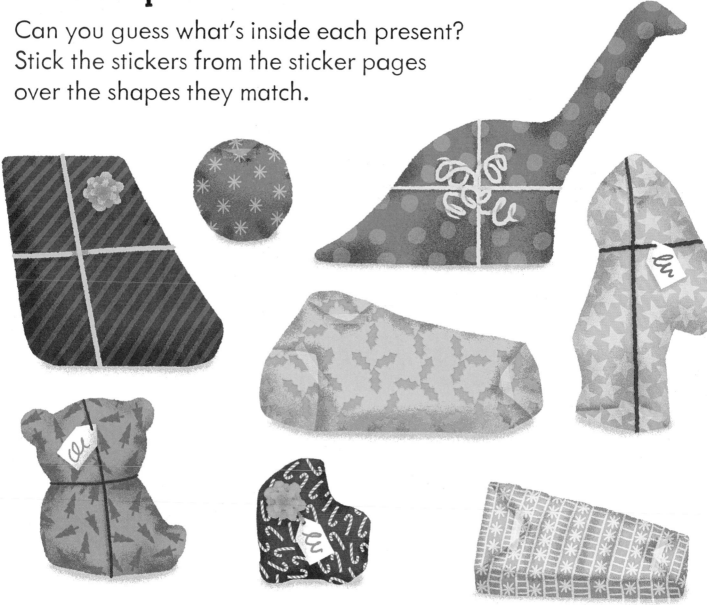

Which gift box is the odd one out?

A   B   C   D

Read Ruby's letter to Santa. Cross out the presents she has already unwrapped. Which one hasn't she opened yet?

Dear Santa,
Please could I have...

colouring pencils
a bike
a skipping rope
building blocks
a train set

Thank you,
Ruby

Are there more spotty or stripy presents?

There are more .... presents.

Ice skating

Can you spot...

...a penguin
wearing a
Santa hat?

...two penguins that
have bumped into
each other?

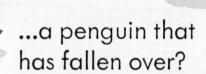

...a penguin that
has fallen over?

How many green
hats can you count? ....

...two penguins
in love?

...a penguin wearing
a Christmas jumper?

Which penguin below
has caught a fish?

A   B   C

Christmas trees

Lily and Thomas are trying to find a Christmas tree. Draw around the tree they're thinking about when you spot it.

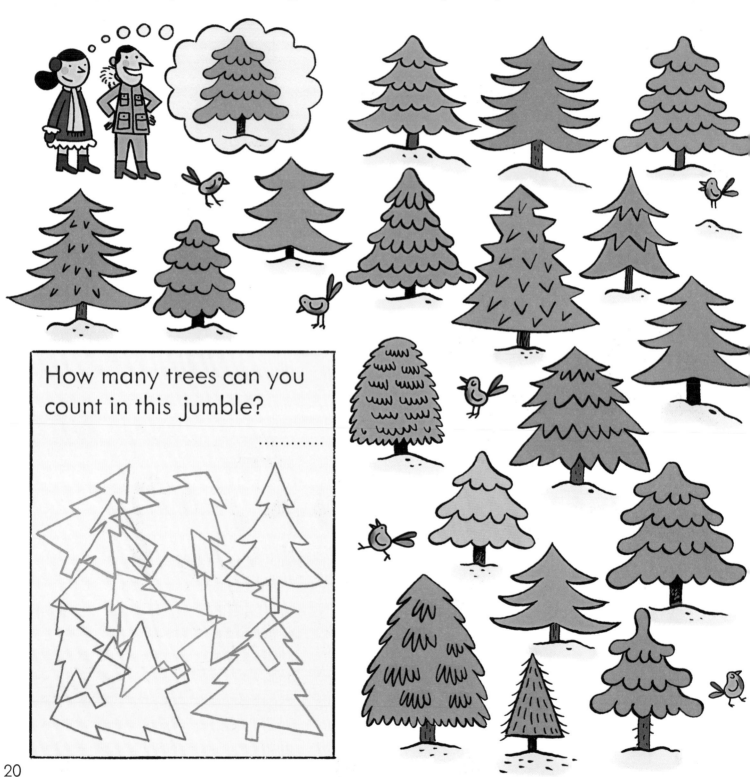

How many trees can you count in this jumble?

....

Decorate this Christmas
tree with stickers from
the sticker pages.

Draw more presents
under the tree.

Winter woodland

Can you spot...

...a reindeer
about to bite a
snowman's nose?

...a hungry
squirrel?

...a sleeping
badger?

...an owl in
a tree hole?

...a fox running
in the snow?

...a rabbit in
its burrow?

Christmas clothes

Match the hats and gloves to these children.
Draw lines between them.

Finish the pattern on this knitted scarf.

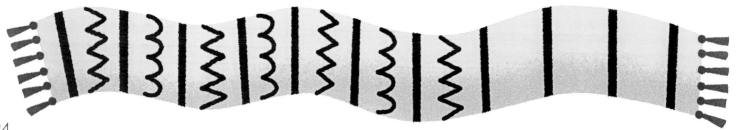

Colour in the pictures on these Christmas jumpers.

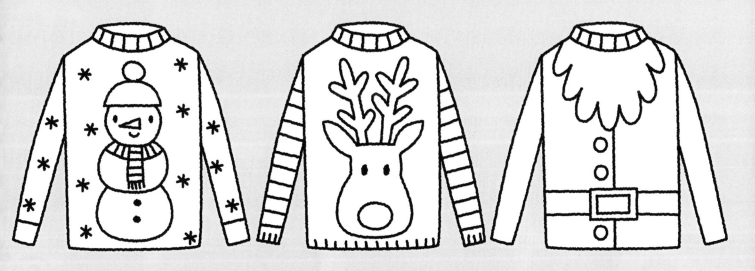

Dress these children using the stickers from the sticker pages.

Christmas stars

Colour in the stars.

Can you find a star with five points on this page?

Draw a line between the two stars in each matching pair.

Join the green stars from 1 to 10. Then, join the brown stars too.

The North Pole

Santa lives at the North Pole. Read the clues then put the sticker of Santa's house (from the sticker pages) in the correct square.

Santa's house is next to...

• his reindeer
• some trees
• his workshop

elf village

Santa's workshop

reindeer stables

sleigh shed

North Pole

Draw a line that leads Twinkle the elf from her house to the workshop. She needs to meet the other elves on her way.

Twinkle

Santa has lost the key to the shed where he keeps his sleigh. Can you find it?

Christmas toys

Can you spot five differences between these nutcracker dolls?

Draw the missing half of this teddy bear.

Which of these Russian dolls doesn't match the others?

Draw a line that takes the toy train past a snowman, two rabbits, an elf and then a reindeer.

How many Christmas trees does the train also go past?

....

Does it go through a tunnel?

YES / NO

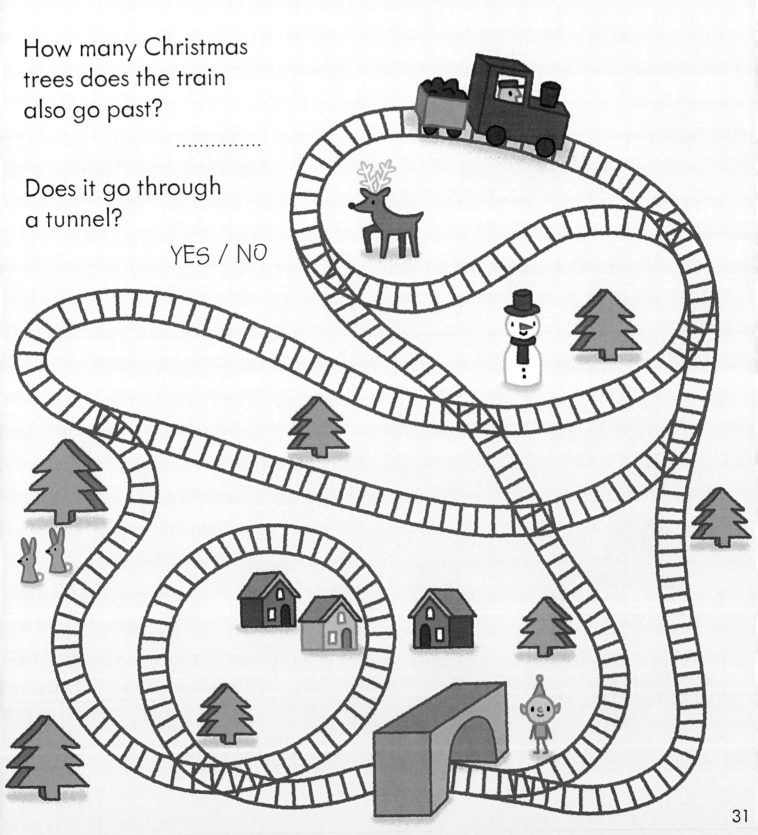

Sticker snowmen

Build lots of snowmen using the different shapes of stickers from the sticker pages.

Use a big circle for a body.

Christmas shopping

Sweet treats

Perfect presents
Pages 16-17

Christmas trees Pages 20-21

The North Pole
Pages 28-29

Santa's house

Christmas clothes Pages 24-25

Sticker snowmen Page 32

Dress Santa... Page 33

Merry birds

Pages 40-41

Christmas Eve

Pages 52-53

Happy New Year

Page 60

Dress Santa and Mrs. Claus

Find hats, coats and boots for Santa and Mrs. Claus on the sticker pages, then stick them on.

Stick Santa's sack here too.

33

Decorations

Which plug is connected to the lights on the Christmas tree?

....

How many fir cones are on each wreath?
Which has the most?

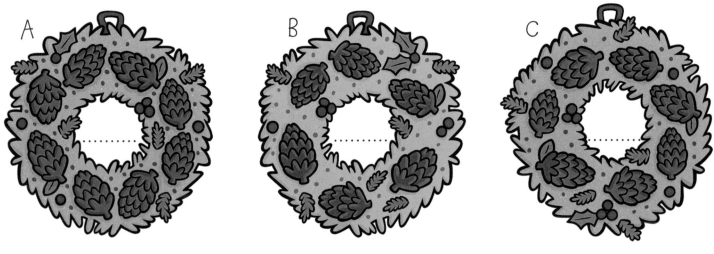

A

B

C

Wreath .... has the most.

Put the bells in their order of size. Write 1 under the smallest bell and 5 under the biggest.

Can you spot five differences? Draw a circle around each one.

Festive fingerprints

Use a black pen to turn these fingerprints into Christmassy pictures.

snowmen

penguins

polar bears

reindeer

elves

birds

37

Santa's holiday

After a busy Christmas, Santa, Mrs. Claus and the elves are taking a break on a tropical island.

Fill in the palm tree's leaves with a green pen.

Bing   Ivy   Elvis

Whose sandals made these footprints? ....

Draw birds in the sky and waves in the sea.

Can you spot a crab?

Which sandcastle is the odd one out?

....

A B C D E

Merry birds

Are there enough berries on the branches on this page for every bird to eat one each?

YES / NO

Can you spot a bird that's singing?

There's something different about one of the birds on this branch. Which one?

A   B   C   D

Which bird has the longest tail feathers?

Find the baby bird stickers on the sticker pages and put each one next to the big bird it matches.

Christmas town

Can you spot ten differences between this picture...

...and this one? Draw a circle around each difference.

Santa's reindeer

It's the reindeers' day off and they're playing in the snow.

Can you spot Rudolph?

Colour in this reindeer's hat.

Doodle more hoof prints in the snow.

Draw antlers on this reindeer.

Are there enough carrots for each reindeer to have one?

YES / NO

This reindeer has lost a bell. Can you find it?

Monster party

The monsters are having a Christmas party. Can you spot...?

• a Santa hat
• a monster singing
• a snowmonster (look carefully)
• a monster wearing antlers
• three straws
• five green balloons

How many blue party
hats can you see?

....

Draw overlapping shapes for paperchains on the orange and pink lines.

Are there enough mini burgers for every monster at the party?

YES / NO

47

Christmas market

Which boy is Jacob? Read the clues, then look for him in the picture.

- Jacob is wearing a hat.
- He has freckles.
- He is on the merry-go-round.

Can you find Mitzi, too?

- She is sitting down.
- She is eating a sausage.

Write an 'X' next to the carol singer who isn't singing.

These shoppers are thinking about what they want to buy. Find each thing and draw around it.

Let it snow

Which picture shows the town before it snowed? ....

A   B   C   D

Snow angels are made by lying on your back and moving your arms and legs. Match everyone to their snow angels.

Add faces to these snowflakes.

Christmas Eve

Put the stocking stickers from the sticker pages below the descriptions they match.

spotty   tartan   biggest   red

milk   carrots   pies

Stick snacks for Santa and his reindeer on the table too.

Santa is on his way and almost everyone in this house is fast asleep. Draw a circle around whoever is still awake.

Santa's journey

Draw a line across these pages leading Santa
to the buildings, in this order:

- house with a green door
- house with a flat roof
- three cottages in a row
- house with five windows
- widest house
- house with two chimneys
- tallest building

Start here

How many reindeer are
pulling Santa's sleigh?

....

Doodle stars in the night sky.

Santa doesn't stop at one house because the people that live there are away this Christmas. Mark it with an 'X'.

Festive fancy dress

Find and colour...

...a snowman's hat and nose

...a dog in costume

...two people in matching costumes

...a present costume

...a penguin

...a star

...someone dressed as a Christmas tree

Colour in the other pictures if you like.

Winter sports

Draw more people riding in the cable cars.

Draw lines between the snowboarders and their matching boards.

This skier scores points for every flag she passes. Add up the numbers on the red, yellow and blue flags. Then, draw a line down the slope that gives her 8 points.

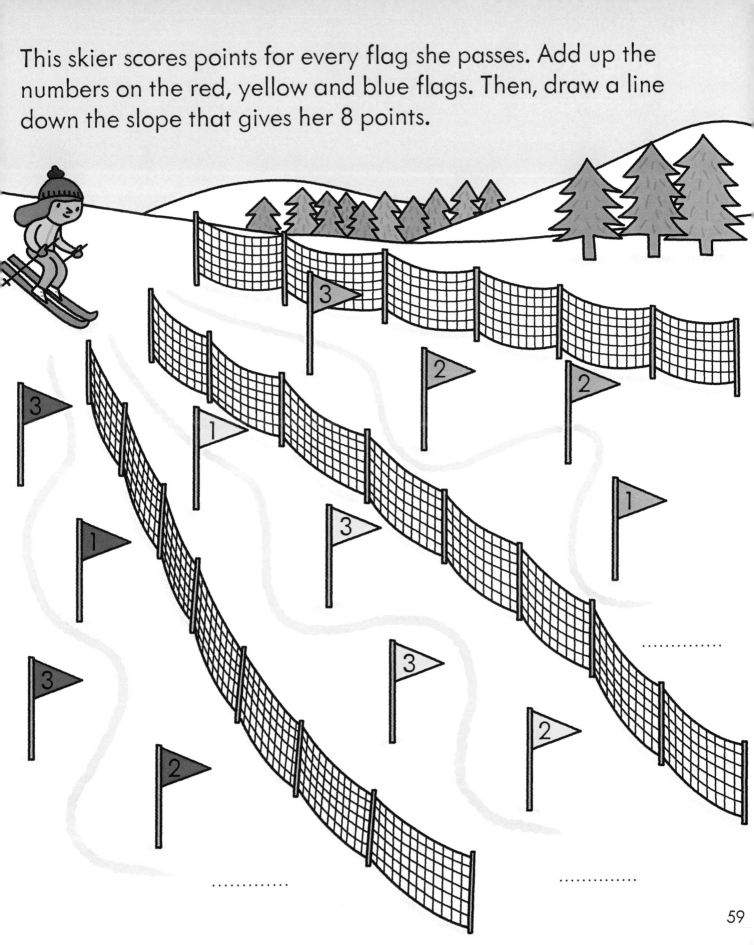

Happy New Year

Use the stickers to fill the sky with fireworks on New Year's Eve.

Answers

2-3 Festive spotting

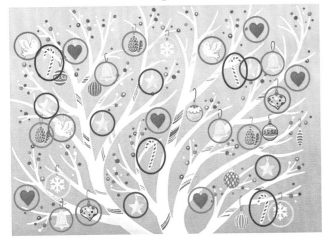

- ○ 6 red hearts
- ○ 3 fir cones
- ○ 3 snowflakes
- ○ 4 candy canes
- ○ 3 white doves
- ○ 4 bells
- ○ 6 gold stars
- ○ 2 spotty decorations

4-5 Christmas shopping

The blue car has the most shopping.

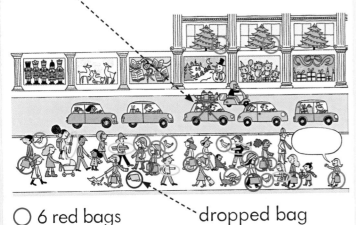

dropped bag

- ○ 6 red bags
- ○ 5 Santa hats
- ○ 6 rolls of paper
- ○ 4 green bags
- ○ 6 pigeons

8-9 Santa's grotto

- ○ clock
- ○ elf in floppy hat
- ○ shopping bags
- ○ yellow star
- ○ sleeping baby
- ○ spotty scarf
- ○ mouse
- ○ 7 presents

10-11 Cool creatures

There are 8 polar bears.

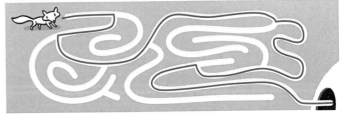

12-13 Sweet treats

Square C is missing from the jar.

14-15 Santa's workshop

ibek = bike
lodl = doll
kobo = book

The sleeping elf is under the book machine.

There are 4 wrapped and 7 unwrapped presents.

16-17 Perfect presents

Present C is the odd one out.

Ruby hasn't opened her building blocks yet.

There are more stripy presents.

18-19 Ice skating

○ penguin wearing a Santa hat
○ penguins bumping into each other
○ penguin that has fallen over
○ penguins in love
○ penguin wearing a Christmas jumper

There are 7 green hats.

Penguin C has caught a fish.

20-21 Christmas trees

There are 9 jumbled Christmas trees.

22-23 Winter woodland

○ deer biting a snowman's nose
○ hungry squirrel
○ sleeping badger
○ owl in a tree hole
○ running fox
○ rabbit in its burrow

24-25 Christmas clothes

26-27 Christmas stars

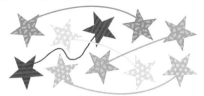

28-29 The North Pole

key

30-31 Christmas toys

The train goes past 6 Christmas trees.

Yes, the train goes through a tunnel.

34-35 Decorations

Plug C is connected to the lights.

Wreath A has the most fir cones.
(A: 8, B: 6, C: 7)

You should number the bells from left to right: 4, 3, 2, 1, 5

38-39 Santa's holiday

Elvis made the footprints.

Sandcastle D is the odd one out.

The crab is next to Mrs. Claus.

40-41 Merry birds

No, there are not enough berries.

Bird C has a red tummy.

○ singing bird

○ longest tail feathers

42-43 Christmas town

44-45 Santa's reindeer

○ Rudolph   ○ lost bell

There are enough carrots for each reindeer.

46-47 Monster party

○ Santa hat   ○ antlers
○ singing monster   ○ straws
○ snowmonster   ○ green balloons
○ 5 blue hats

No, there are not enough burgers.

48-49 Christmas market

○ Jacob   ○ Mitzi

This singer isn't singing.

50-51 Let it snow

Picture D shows the town before it snowed.

52-53 Christmas Eve

The boy in the top bunk bed is awake.

54-55 Santa's journey

9 reindeer are pulling the sleigh.

empty house

58-59 Winter sports

The blue flags give the skier 8 points.

First published in 2016 by Usborne Publishing Ltd., Usborne House, 83-85 Saffron Hill, London EC1N 8RT, England. www.usborne.com © 2016 Usborne Publishing Ltd. The name Usborne and the devices ♀ ⊕ are Trade Marks of Usborne Publishing Ltd. All rights reserved. No part of this publication may be reproduced, stored in a retrieval system or transmitted in any form or by any means, electronic, mechanical, photocopying, recording or otherwise without the prior permission of the publisher. UKE.